darling

heather leigh

ISBN (paperback):
ISBN (ebook):

Edits by: Jocelyn Carbonara and Jeff Alessandrelli
Cover design and illustrations by: Mia Marie Overgaard
Page design and typesetting by: Paul Baillie-Lane

Honorable mention of "If My Heart Were A Home"
in Broadcast A Collection of Canadian Poems.

Contents

Dedicated to those who have saved me without realizing they were the ones who could save me.

The
Withering
Mind

Morning Mourning

Grief clings onto her
    Like a drenched, washed-out, smothering T-shirt—
    Sticking to every piece of skin,
    Engulfing the entirety of her skeleton.

Shouting for Sorrow

Sorrow leaves her coarse and numb.

Most days, it hides amongst the shadows, only to come out and play when the earth drapes

    in black, and freckles of stars dance over the sky.

Other days, sorrow invades her airways,

Emptying her of joy whenever it so desires.

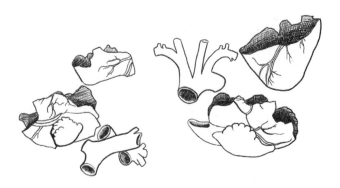

Selfish

She was the type
who broke her own heart
before letting others
grab hold of the pieces
and break it for themselves.

I Am a Prisoner of My Own Mind

You etch yourself deep beneath my skin,
Slither through my brain.

Wrapping your torturous breath around my thoughts.
You wreak panic upon the air as it tangles itself into knots
   too tight to escape my lungs.

You force my hands to turn as cold as dry ice,
Forming a tenacious entanglement of worry to awaken deep in
   the pit in my stomach.

Your name, my friend, is anxiety, and
I cannot break free from your embrace.

Trying to Find the Light When I Am Drowning in Darkness

When the clouds cry sprinkles of diamonds,

And the sun no longer confides in the moon.

When the sky bleeds into nightfall,

And obscurity engraves itself into the fractures of my stained-
    glass heart—

Stripping away the light that once formed all my vehemence.

I have turned gray,

Like the nights when December rains.

Haunted

Your ghostly grasp still wraps itself around my throat.
Smothering me from clear air.
Charred remains are left for only me to see.

Tell me: why did you abandon your debris to collapse all over me?

Even though I tried so damn hard to leave you in the past,
And even though you did not leave a single mark on me—
You made me believe I was unworthy of love.

You shattered all of me with just one haunted breath when you
purred hello in the depths of my mind.

Battle Within

Her mind was filled with darkness,
But her soul was filled with light.
It was a battle between her mind and her heart,
With no knowledge of which one would conquer.

Bad Things Always Happen
When Happiness Is Involved

I feel I am cemented to the inside of a casket that I have built all
    on my own—
Four translucent walls strangling my mind.

I fear if I step outside my casket and grab hold of the happiness,
I will disintegrate into fragments of my own remains;
I may perish into the rhythm of the wind,
So I trap myself inside—
Inside this casket I have fabricated.

I brought with me a diminutive amount of happiness to sustain me,
Believing it would not be replaced by some melancholy like the rest.

This casket becomes my safe haven.

Healing Reflections

You only show your pain
When tears of glass puncture your skin's surface, and
Darkness screams at the moon.

You only show your pain,
When the mirror is your only friend awake, and
Your reflection confesses you must be healed.

Coping Mechanism

A beautiful disaster she is;
Fragile memories fracture the soul that barely remains,
Coping with dismay by shutting herself off,
Whispering to her shadows to feel less alone.
Her mind is a delicate sculpture,
Unaware of when it may implode.

Am I Destructing My Own Self?

Are you the one gently drowning me, forcing me to inhale a galaxy too vast and liquid to fit within my feeble lungs?

Or am I the one holding the stars and drinking their poison until it immerses itself into every organ—leaving my heart to dissipate before it can open up to you?

A Breakup Letter to My Depression

I wanted to love how you…

Caress my brain with the calluses of your dominant fingers,
Infect my thoughts with your lamenting breath,
Indulge in the agony that sweats from my pores,
Cradle my heart so tightly it soon will shatter,
Compose your name within the scars on my skin—obsessed
  with yourself.

Blue is your favourite colour—the same colour that paints my
emptiness and drips from my wet eyes—
So please go away and never return.
I could never, and will never,
Love you
  The same way you consume me.

Misery Is Your Only Friend

You wear sadness well…

Resting on your shoulders like a Gucci purse,
It carves out your curves like your favourite summer dress
when you dance under the moon,
Drapes over your knees like your nightgown when you hide
deep beneath your bedding.

You wear sadness embroidered in the stitches of your favourite
sweater.
And your collarbone is stained with droplets of mascara.

You wear sadness almost too well.

Last Hurrah

My heart ceases to pump
Galaxies into my veins.
My bones are drained,
Eroding into crystals.

Fold my paper lungs
Into a thousand paper planes,
And allow me to breathe in this universe one last time.

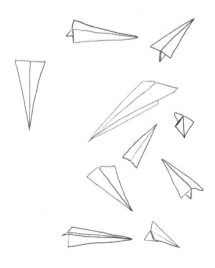

Hopelessly Here

Feeling nothing is worse than feeling something;
It is the repetitive heartbeat that goes unnoticed.

Tears stuck to the back of your throat,
Your mind submerged in black waves
Drowns the knowledge of pain.

Until mildew grows amongst your lungs,
Your legs tingle, and then your fingers and toes.

It's a feeling you never want to stop,
Because you felt it.

But it soon fades,
And your fingers cease to remind you they're there.
Your legs begin to work,
But your mind is unaware of the direction they're heading.
You blend into the wallpaper,
Unaware of your own existence.

You'd rather feel something than continue to feel nothing at all.

Blue

"Please let my body feel again,"
She pleaded to no one in particular.
She has been calling out for help,
But no one seems to hear
As her voice turns to dust.

She has been calling out for help,
But the words get stuck to the lining of her windpipe.
Suffocating in silence,
She prays to let all this pain go.

Killer

It is not alcohol.
It is not the drugs.
It is my own damn mind
Slowly killing me.

Blame

Droplets of mold linger amidst the cracks of my once-porcelain skin,

Each bone crumbles against another,

My vision rusts with dishonesty,

My organs drown in self-pity,

Lungs sprout weeds instead of flowers,

Grief flutters through my stale veins, back into my heart,

My body is decaying,

And only my thoughts are to blame.

Finding Shelter

I am battling the constant grenade of my mind,

Knowing it could detonate at any moment.

But the chance of winning the battle is worth enduring the

inconsequential rubble left behind.

Will You Sink or Swim?

If your mind is slowly sinking,
Do you fight to fill the hole before water submerges the ship,
Or allow the sea to drown your soul?

I Bleed Misery

Happiness has drained from my veins.

Instead of galaxies, my heart is made of black holes.

I bleed misery, even when life gives me victories;
I bleed bitterly, even when life hits me with gorgeous deliveries.

Flying doesn't sound so bad, until I hit the ground;
Maybe flying won't feel so bad, when I no longer hit the ground.

Silent Suffering

Sometimes I don't feel the strength to talk.
I'd rather just cave into the misery of my thoughts—
Allowing darkness to shadow against the lining of my skull—
Because explaining my mind
Is more painful than swallowing my tongue.

Lungs Threaded with Desolation

If you reach down my throat,
The only thing you will be able to grasp is the loneliness that
dances within my lungs.

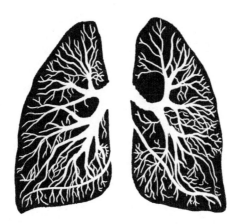

Emotional Chaos

The highs take me past the moon to a galaxy of euphoria.

My lows drown my lungs in cement, allowing no room to breathe.

There is never an in-between.

I Walked Through Hell
Without Getting Burnt

If anyone deserves to dance amongst this earth's soil,
It is me.
You have not seen the darkness that draped my soul,
Like a veil to blind me of light.
I have sunk deeper than rock bottom;
I have picked my teeth with bigger monsters than you;
My flesh has bled scarier entities than you;
I have met the devil;
He dances with me in my sleep.

Depression on Display

I am suffocating in my own head;
The air around my brain thickens;
I feel I am trapped in a glass jar,
Sealed shut with no holes to breathe.
Everyone is staring at me as if I am on display—
A darkened soul in a world of sunshine.

SOS

What do her eyes reveal?
Do they glisten with grief?
Do her lips gush with secrets—
Amidst her soul intertwined with darkness?

Her mind dances with the devil,
But she hopes her skin masks the loneliness beating within her heart.

Are you fooled by her disguise,
Or can you hear her whispers for help—
Her yearning for a chance to heal?

Wallpaper in a Darkened Room

Sometimes my soul feels a little misplaced,

Even when I am surrounded by people who adore me.

I feel I should blend within the walls,

For my mind whispers

I will forever be alone.

The Scream Silences
the Kindness

When I look at my reflection,
My flaws scream back,
Filling my heart with hatred.
I see the places that are broken,
The places filled with disgust.

While other times my reflection,
Is a gentle hand,
Pressed against my cheek—
Oh so beautiful.

But the harsh reality is
No matter how hard I look,
The scream is louder than the gentle touch.

Dancing with Depression

You smother me like a wet blanket,
Dripping mold of resentment against my skin.
You fasten my lungs with misery,
Until they no longer seek air.
You twirl me so gracefully,
Until dizziness blurs my vision.
You try to be gentle,
But your hands suffocate my windpipe.
You have taught me to dance with you,

You show no mercy,
No sign of letting go.
I have become so reliant on the dance
That I am afraid I will fall without you.
Who am I without you—
Without this anguish?

My Brain Reveals Sadness

I am trapped in the darkest room
With no way for light to enter,
Bound to a pain only my brain can comprehend.

Bleeding and Pleading

Most days I don't want to get out of bed.
It's like cotton has stuck to the back of my throat.
My mind is working in overdrive,
But my body moves aimlessly
To the rhythm of this daily routine.
I'm screaming for help,
But my voice is drowning in sorrow,
Silencing the weight of this depression.

Another Sip to Darkness

When wine drops onto my tongue,
It swells two sizes too big,
Suffocating my airway,
Making it so I cannot breathe.

When vodka drips into my veins,
My blood dries instantly,
Breaking apart all my closed wounds,
Ripping me open.

I tell myself alcohol will cure me,
Make the darkness evaporate,
So I pour another glass
And immerse my organs in liquid courage.

But when the alcohol reaches my brain,
My pain returns,
Only this time twice as gruesome as before,
Because I cannot silence it.
I only awaken the pain that has been there all along.

Solitary Confinement Within
My Own Skin

Loneliness has begun eroding my skeleton.

Each bone in my body aches as empty promises leave them to
disintegrate.

I have no one in a city filled with millions,

So I watch the stars dance amongst the midnight air,

And let my lonely tears make water-colour paintings within the
darkened sky.

I Am Self-Destructive

I yearn to plant seeds in my lungs,

Allow flowers to sprout amidst my heart,

Their stems transform my veins.

But I always tend to drown my garden

With tears of salt—

Tearing the roots from their soil,

Never giving them the chance to breathe—

Choking them of the air they deserve.

Because if my garden heals,

Grows,

That means I must too.

And that is more terrifying than re-pollinating seeds every year

And shredding their petals before they can bloom.

Stranger Inside My Head

I can feel the marrow of my skull singing,
Soft and gentle, trying to show me grace as it grows against my
    throat.
Each rhythmic beat caresses my bitter blood.
Who is this stranger singing lullabies to convert stone to art,
Healing my fragile brain with joy, erasing envy, and sprouting
    flowers amidst my brain?
This stranger with the velvet-dipped voice is no stranger at all—
Just my own heartbeat, trying to fix my cracked soul.

Anxious Dreams

I'm in a state of constant déjà vu,
My heart pulsing to the beat of hopelessness
In a never-ending cycle of worrying over the feeling of
    something terrible happening.
Is my brain wired incorrectly?
Or is my world about to turn upside down?

Reusable

I recycle old smiles,

So no one can see that my mind is eroded with pain.

Will I ever be the same as someone whose brain is not strung
with faulty wires?

So I recycle old smiles

And hope no one notices the difference between the two.

Fading
Heart

Hesitancy

I laid in bed with him
and thought of you.

No Going Back

How do you rebuild a puzzle with a few missing pieces?
How do you grasp onto mist once it seeps through your fingertips?
How do you rebuild love once your trust runs out?
You don't.

I'm Already Broken

Months after you died
When the phone would howl,
My heart would pause
      with each deafening ring.
Air would tangle around my lungs—
      a terror that seemed so insignificant.

I could not mourn another person;
My soul could not withhold another crack.

Take Me, Not Her

Her urn was sculpted from marble.

Bury me in the ground,
Not her.
Dissolve the marble that I would rest in,
Not the soul that has been laid to rest.
Allow the sun to radiate onto her porcelain skin once again,
And make the soil to drain over mine.

But that is why she vowed to be cremated,
So I could not take her place—
because she knew I would.

Just One Last Embrace

In my dreams,

I dance with your ghost.

It is the only time

I can still feel your embrace.

When my eyes rest,

I fool myself into believing that heaven did not take you away.

My dreams are the only time when the whispering ache of

    losing you dims.

So I will continue dancing with your ghost for as long as I can.

Existing

Infatuated with our past,
Success drips from our tongues;
We chase after moments
Like fireflies fading.

We forget how to be together,
Because it's easier to reminisce
About memories we've already lived,
Than to create something from the
unfamiliarity of each new day.

If we ever went back to our past,
Instead of re-living the alluring memories embedded into our minds,
We'd have so much
We'd want to change.

Unquenchable Hunger

I crave to meet a man who makes me feel the same way
poetry does.

Wasp Stings

Betrayal is the feeling of a
    swarm of wasps
    nesting inside her throat,
each word pricking against her raw windpipe—begging to escape.

She felt like the sun had shattered against her chest, leaving
darkness to erode each harrowing breath.

Lessons to Learn

My heart is filled with glass,

    translucent,

    each shard pieced together

    by a wool thread—

    the strands fraying amongst the weight.

I allow others to see

    too much of me—

    their reflection of me burning the wool thread

    until it disintegrates,

    and the glass pieces shatter

    against my ribcage.

He Watched Her Diminish
and Didn't Give a Damn

The problem was she was trying so hard to keep the love alive.
But love cannot grow without a little rain,
    a little nurturing.
And he was only willing to supply her with a drought,
Leaving the love to wither away.

Affirmed Affection

Her trust is made of glass, cracked with affirmation.
Her beauty and transparency will gradually shatter,
And those tainted shards will impale the rest of her.

Six Feet Under

Here lies the body of the love of my life,
The soul of the woman who fought too hard for less than
  she deserved.
Rest in peace.
To those who took her for granted,
Decaying the beauty amidst her heart,
Her heaven will be a love without betrayal.

Not My Safe Haven

You were supposed to be my safe place.

I was supposed to run towards you when pain struck.

But with each passing day,

I am running from you,

Because you are the one causing me so much pain.

The Butterflies Are Dying

The butterflies are only moments away from perishing;
With tattered wings unwilling to fly,
They have starved themselves of euphoria,
Hopelessly trying to survive.

He does not give her the fluttery sensation of tender wings
quivering against the lining of her stomach.

Now she just feels their carcasses laying to rot in the emptiness;
And with him, she is only left with loneliness.

Taking Advantage

I was your training wheels,
But you already knew how to ride a bike.

Weather Changes,
Guilt Is Forever

When the sky weeps,
And you self-reflect amidst the heavy downfall.
The hole in your umbrella begins to drip droplets of misery onto
　　your forehead.

Know that I do not feel a twinge of pain for you.

You were the one who made it rain shards of glass;
You cut open my soul and left me bleeding self-doubt.
I hope your bones will shiver with the guilt of losing me,
Even when the sky stops mourning.

He Feeds on Her Pain

He licks her wounds
    with a salty tongue.
Her paper lungs
    burn in his animosity.
Blood trickles
    outside of her heart.

And all he will do
    is lie down to watch.

You Are My Misery

I have soared through burning skies,
Swam through oceans filled with my tears,
Climbed out of devastating pits,
And hid from my own happiness
Just to find the root of my misery.

It was not the voices screaming into my brain, or the anxiety
Keeping me awake.
It was the letters that spelt out your name.

Your Heart Is No Longer for Me

Where do you go
When you go quiet,
When your mind turns
     to other women,
When your heart no longer beats
     to the rhythm of mine?

What are you hiding from me
When your eyes grow hollow, and your lips drip another name?

Where do I go
After my heart pours onto the floor?

I go right back to you—
The boy who will never turn into the man of my dreams.

Why Her and Not Me?

I think of love
as a weed,
growing where forbidden,
searching for the sun,
intertwining
with the thorns of a rose—
disguising the red of its petals,
only to be unmasked
after trying too hard to blend in.

Why didn't you choose me?
Was I the soil in your garden,
and is she the rose blooming so beautifully amidst it?

Desolation

I've held my breath for months in the sleek dark of night;
My lungs sprouted from the moon.

Who am I kidding?
I've choked on my breath for months in the light of day;
I'm unable to sustain clean air.

Shrinking myself from those who love me most,
I deflate my heart with self-sabotage;
My lungs can no longer withstand the weight of your vacant promises.

I'm rotting from my core, and there is no one else to blame but you.

Renege

A man of promise
is not always a man of his word.

Monsters Disguised as Friends

It's funny how someone can
Break into a relationship and tear one person to shreds,
Burying them alive with a choice they made—
While still staring at their own reflection and
Loving themselves unapologetically.

Temporary Fixations

Grief sedated by orgasms;
Orgasms sedated by grief.

A tiresome circle,
A reprieve from pain,
Only to be left in more agony.

Because sex
Cannot bring them back,
Cannot fill emptiness,
Cannot heal wounds.

Drowning in This Galaxy

My heart is heavy,

A cement block drifting to the pit of my heart.

How can it keep weighing me down,

When there is nothing left of it to hold onto?

Surrendering

My everything was never going to be enough for you, yet
Your promises sounded so authentic,
Melting from your tongue like salted caramel.

I saw the red flags,
Swaying to the rhythm of our silence.
Days on end,
You would leave me in silence.
Days on end,
My head was drowning in my own tears.

But then you would reappear,
And lust or love, I did not care;
My heart could not give up on us—
Until red was the only colour I saw from you,
Until my everything meant nothing to you,
Until you left me shattered on the ground.

Foolish to believe you could ever reciprocate the love I gave to you,
I could never be enough for you.

And now as I heal my own wounds,
I am thankful,
Because you were the colour red,
And my favourite colour is blue.

A Home Built Within You

I built a home in you,
Remember?
My essence is the structure of your heart.
I am embedded within the cells of your brain
How could you forget me?

Restless

My lungs reach for my windpipe
As I scream your name.
The clouds roll their eyes for another night,
Listening to the howl of my cries.

Are you even listening?

I miss you.
I need you.
I have always needed you,
And I always will.

You Will Remember Me No Matter How Hard You Try Not to

When you wash the day off your hands,
You will still see my soul on your palms—cracked and crumbled.

The day may rinse off your hands,
But the pain you've caused me never will.

My heart lies in all of your debris.

Lost Oxygen

Your breath tastes of last night's cigarette,
As looming hearts submerge under waves of lost feelings.
Your eyes gaze beyond me.
Maybe at the women behind me?
I watch the tip of your newly lit cigarette kindle,
The spark igniting with each inhale—
Like how I inhaled you.
But soon, the spark suffocates from lack of oxygen,
As our spark has over and over again,
And I watch the embers fade out.

Some days, I crave the taste of last night's cigarette,
But I remember I was suffocating within the smoke.

Do You See Happiness?

When I look into your eyes,
I see a sunrise, pastel happiness.
But I wonder what you see
when you look into mine?

Meaningless

What runs through your mind
When she is not enough for you?
What bodies are you craving?
What voices form your rhythm?
As you figure out your perfect woman,
She will be left to drown in your mistakes.

Thoughts Amidst
The Early Mornings

Broken people
Break people too.

Mockery

I write to forget you,
But the irony is, with each word,
I am reminded of you.
So am I really writing to forget you,
Or to ensure that I can't forget you?

Thin Connection

I've been dancing on telephone wires,
Hoping the communication is still electric;
But at the end of the day,
You never pick up the phone when I call,
No matter how steadily I dance.

You Chose Lust Over Love

It's starting to get bad again.
I can feel it gnawing at the lining of my skull—
The idea of your body on top of her.
Her moans heavily drape the night sky—
Smothering my brain night and day.

Will forgiveness ever drip down my throat again,
Quenching my pain?
Will I ever be able to look you in the eyes and not see hers
    staring back at me?
Will my soul forever be hollowed?

My bones lie emptied of trust—
Unanswered questions surging through my veins.
Why was my love not good enough,
But her lust was?

Selfish Remorse

She is so broken,
Her eyes hollowed.
He made her this way.

He tells her he is full of remorse—
Words weeping from his lips—
But his eyes are screaming
He doesn't care.
Her pain is not his pain,
So why should he own it?

Her pain is not his pain,
Because he couldn't handle it if it were.

She is the one full of remorse
For loving someone who loved himself more than he could ever
    love her.

Love Became Hard When You Bruised My Heartstrings

Resenting you has become easier
than loving you.

Losing Game

You manipulated me into believing everything was my fault,
I was the one to blame,
Even when my heart was shattered against the cement floor,
And yours was still whole.

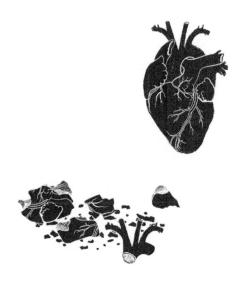

She Got the Best Version of You

I feel the most pain when I see you with her,

Not because you have moved on,

Or because I am envious of her.

I feel the most pain because you treat her like she is the soil
   that feeds your soul,

Yet you treated me like I was nothing but the dirt you stomped upon.

Battlefield

My tongue drips resentment,
But my heart still envisions love.
It is a constant fight between a reflective misconception
And the reality that you would drown me in.

Bleeding Love

It is certain you have drained me to my core,
And that's when I knew I loved too deeply—
When my entire existence bled the need to love harder,
Even for the ones like you,
Who couldn't bear the love I already offered.

Lenience

Sometimes I wish I could hold you,
Wish I could feel your touch,
But the betrayal you've caused me
Makes it unbearable to meet your eyes—
Your beautiful eyes are filled only with lies.

Sometimes I wish I could go back to the day we met,
When your smile blossomed hope into my lungs.
But you cannot take back the words you did not say,
When your body wants to betray.

Sometimes I wish I could hear you say you're sorry.
But I have learned to forgive the silence gasping for air.
I have learned to forgive you, to better myself.
I have made peace with the broken pieces.

Yearning Sentiment

I sometimes get homesick for your hands,
Which don't even want to hold me.
You praise yourself like you grew flowers amongst my flesh,
But you left no array of roses to sprout amidst this moss-filled body.

I was afraid I'd never find a love like you,
But the moment I realized I lost myself in a garden of weeds
Was the moment I realized I found someone who would grow
meadows amongst my bones.
And that somebody was me.

I Gave My Last Breath
to Refill Your Lungs

What I would give to hear your voice again…

I would give away the universe that drips beneath my feet.

I would give away the butterflies that ripple between my lungs.

I would give away the mountains that paint my backyard and
the oceans that fuel my soul.

I would give away the world just to hear your voice again—

Because your voice has been fading,

And I cannot allow myself to let it vanish completely.

Rooted to the Ground

You had all of heaven with me,
But you chose not to learn how to fly.

I soared,
While you were cemented to the lonely soil below.

You could have had heaven,
If you only gave me the time
To teach you how to fly.

They Broke Her

She cannot fathom
A man who worships her.

She cannot fathom
A love that is not based on her body.

She cannot fathom
A man who continues to love her after months pass,
Because she was allured by the men who were already halfway
out the door—
Before introductions were made
Or her name left her lips.

Lost Love

All the love letters that drown my floor
Will not make up for the love you
Flooded elsewhere
And never returned.

Fear of Rejection

As your glass kiss shatters against my flesh,

I choke on my words piercing through my throat.

Goodbye is a noun that doesn't easily escape my lips,

Especially when directed at you.

I try to just spit it out,

But the fear of loneliness suffocates my windpipe;

So instead I just turn and walk away—

Goodbye dissipating in the air behind me.

Dismay

Do I regret giving you every piece of my heart?
No.
Because I am overflowing with love that you so desperately
needed.
Am I disappointed that you got to hold my heart in your hands,
While listening to someone else breathe your name?
Am I disappointed that some other girl has my heart woven into
her lungs—Etched with pieces of me I can never retrieve?

Yes.

Companionship

Do you love them,
Or are you only in love with their company?

I Want a Warranty on My Heart

Why do you miss someone
Who hurt you so severely?
Is it because they still have your heart in their lungs—
Never returning it when they walked away?

The Real Me May
Make You Run Away

What if one day you break through my flesh
And see me
The way that I see myself—
Broken,
Unfixable—
And you leave like all the rest?

Fixated to My Heart

My lungs are coated in smoke,
My liver is marinated in red wine,
But nothing can abolish the thought of you.

I Arrive to My Own Funeral

I wear black to signify the loss of a loved one—
The loss of myself,
Who I mourn in the depths of you.

Red Flags Can Never
Change Colour

You are not the only one to blame.

I thought I could mend those red flags,

Dye them a shade of affection,

But I was wrong.

Those flags were tainted with the devil's lipstick,

And no amount of longing could fade its cruel red.

Dazed Misery

One day when the city lights reflect into your car window,
I hope you think of me,
And realize you lost a piece of yourself that no one could replace—
No matter how hard they try.

Three Little Words Worth
a Thousand Tears

I have written about you at least a thousand times,

A thousand different ways,

Said I love you a thousand times a day,

And thought maybe you would say it back—

Even if it is once in my lifetime—

Because you are worth the thousand words I plead per day.

You Have Carved My Carcass with Violation

When I told you what happened,

You told me it was all in my head.

But the way his cultivating hands slid under my shirt.

Rotted my memories away.

I could form the way his hands preyed against my flesh.

You never believed me,

Even though I told him no.

You made me believe my mind was corrupting,

Even when his tongue went places that were forbidden.

So at a young age I was trained into silence.

I will lock this secret away until it makes me bleed.

Break My Heart Cruelly, Not Cowardly

I would prefer you to reach into the crevice of my heart with
your bare hands
And snap my heartstrings in two,
Then watch me break down from afar.
I thought after all you put me through,
After all this time,
That the least that you owed me was
Not to break my heart in cowardly ways.

Separated Strangers

We are like two foreign objects,

Strangers to the touch,

With two hearts that know too much.

Infidelity Breaks the Strongest Souls

I sometimes still find myself wondering
What it was like to be on top of another,
With her breath against your throat,
Her heart beating against your bare skin,
While I was waiting at home—
Trying to help you grow.

Expose Yourself

Tell them you promised to stitch up all of my wounds,
But instead you took my heart and stuffed its shattered pieces
    into your voids.

Tell them you took my numerous chances
And used them to your advantage.

Tell them you watched my tears bleed onto the floor
And used them to wash away your guilt.

Tell them you used my beautiful soul;
Tell them you used me up whole.

Demolition of My Trust

I think what makes me hate you the most
Is that I never would have done those things you did to me
With such ease,
Such grace.

I Was the Darkness,
She Is Your Sun

I would've walked across shattered glass,

Swam through cement,

Traveled amongst the stars and drowned in each black hole,

To feel like I was good enough for you,

To keep you from seeking attention from others.

I would've danced along electric wires,

Jumped through flaming seas,

To fight this loneliness that you injected into me.

You were my entire world,

While I was your darkest night,

And she is your sun.

Caught Between the Pieces

My heart says to forgive you,
While my brain says to forget you,
And I am torn between the two.

Desolation

My tears taste of emptiness,
My lips taste of loneliness,
And my heart yearns for forgiveness.

Narcissist

My world was wrapped around you,
Enveloped by the need to fix your broken pieces,
Show you how love really is.

But your world was wrapped around yourself,
And I cannot fix you
Until you are ready to fix yourself.

And that is not my job anymore,
So good luck.

We Are So Different

I apologized to you,
While you made my heart weep.
I took the blame for your mistakes,
When I knew damn well I could never do those things to you.

You broke me,
While I continued to build you up;
And that is the difference between the two of us.

I would have given you my broken pieces over and over again
To watch you shatter the shards even more,
While you could easily have watched me break my own heart
And not felt an ounce of remorse.

Are You in Love, Or Do You Want to Be Loved?

Maybe you're in love with the idea of being in love,
And what you're experiencing isn't truly love at all.

Blossoming
Soul

Let Go, to Grow

She gifted dignity to the minds
    that tore her heart apart,
And that liberation is what encouraged her to blossom.

To My Father

You are the man who taught me
    how to rise above the debris
    left for me to suffocate within.
You are the man who does everything
    for everyone else before yourself.
You show me how to be selfless;
You paint colours within my blackened world;
You feed me wisdom.
You are who I seek to be one day
    for my children, friends and family.
You are the man who guided me
    past agony, mending my armor
    when it became dented.
You are the man I will always love.
You are the father many dream for;
I get the privilege to have you as mine.

He Is My Home

Sunbeams reflect against his tender skin
Like light piercing through windows.
Radiating love through the clouds.

As hope drips from his lips,
His weather reminds me of home.

If My Heart Were a Home

Fear of defeat drapes itself against the stained-glass windows,
    blocking radiant colours from carving shadows on the walls.

Clarity materializes from the dim walls,
    only when the haze of anguish—
    seething through the cracks—
    threatens structural damage.
Even after repairs, the cracks would allow remnants of haze to
    grasp the wooden floorboards, convinced no more devastation
    could be done.
The roof would occasionally drip incertitude onto the already
    weakened floors, causing them to fracture into fragments of
    dread and undeniable forgiveness.
Second chances and hopelessness hibernate beside one
    another, until an occupant gives a gentle knock on the locked
    front door.

But when the sun can escape between the drapes, it illuminates
    the darkened intramural vines of beauty rising along the walls,
    entangling themselves in purity.

The aroma of blooming and nourished flowers burst through
    the house,
    destroying fragments of debris left by self-misery.

If my heart were a home, few could brave the hurricane that awakened the sentiments inside.

Love Rooted from Commitment

His smile rooted infatuation within her heart;

His mind flourished security under her soul;

His words grew courage into her mind that once feared itself;

His arms became a home she immersed into whenever the
cruel world became too bitter.

He was the water nourishing her prosperity,

And she was the colour painting him from those who left him
bleeding gray.

Reconstructing Her Heart

He delicately deconstructed the blockade she had built inside
    her heart,
Planting seeds where debris once embedded.

With his patience, the roots will flourish,
Vining into a meadow amongst a heart that no longer needs to
    guard itself
    against tenebrosity and rain.

You Can Awaken the Sky

You darling
inspire the stars
to dance
across the abandoned sky
awakening the lonely moon
to dance
the night away
with you.

Forgive to Forget
or Forget to Forgive?

She attempted to forget, which made her strong.
But she chose to forgive, which made her indestructible.

I Found the Burning Hunger II

You make me feel more than the words that suffocate my heart.
You make me feel the same way poetry does.

You Are the Caretaker
of This Garden

Stop planting yourself in soiled soil
Where your growth will disintegrate
And you will wither without the chance to
Bloom.

Don't Let Her Go

She is a rare finding;
    She will paint your world with vivid colours.
    But once she slips away,
    Those colours will melt to dim shades of gray,
And you will bleed with remorse.

Knit Yourself Into My Heart

You're tangled within my soul, and I wouldn't want it any other way;
    So please, don't untie the pieces of yourself that you have
        woven within me.
    We have knitted our broken pieces together.
    It would be a disarray of knots and loose yarn shedding apart.
    Even without you with me, there will always be a woven
        piece of myself attached to you.

Be Patient with Her

Loving her is like loving
a worn-down house on the verge of collapsing.
Loving her is like staring
at your reflection for hours and hating everything that stares
    back at you.

Loving her is like smashing
a glass masterpiece and trying to glue the pieces partially
    together.

Loving her will be like making
flowers bloom out of a dust filled windowpane—reaching for the
    sunlight, trying to thrive.

Loving her will feel like witnessing
sunbeams glistening off a translucent lake, reviving the cold
    body of water.

As long as you will wait for her love
to etch itself inside your heart,
she will end up giving you every last drop of love she has left.

Because
loving her is
patiently beautiful.

Against All Odds

For once, I think I may stay.
For once, I may not run in fear.

For once, my world does not feel hopelessly grey.

For once, happiness is so near.

I will give you the best of me,
The rest of me,
And everything in between,
Because for once, I will stay.

He Grew Love in a Place
Where Love Had Been Lost

He tore down the stained-glass windows,
Filling her sheltered soul with light.

He dismantled the barricade surrounding her heart,
Rebuilding the fractured pieces with patience.

He showed her how to be loved perfectly,
Cherishing her crumbling soul
Until she transformed into a flourishing masterpiece of infatuation.

Winter's Love

The branches lay bare, like her skin on his.
Ice cold hands tangled themselves in each other;
Snowflake eyes glazed with purity reflected up at her with
   glaciers of love;
Happiness thawed from the frozen water body—
Reviving the love that winter tried to numb.

Those Who Remain Do
Not Need Us to Beg

I will not beg to be loved.

I will not beg for less than I deserve.

I am not a charity case kneeling down upon great ones.

I am divine.

I will never again beg for someone who does not see the gold
that drips from my heart.

A Message to My Younger Self

Little girl…
You do not need to
please everybody
you come across.

You do not need to
change yourself
for any boy's attention;
the right one will gravitate
towards the real you.

Be confident;
your personality outshines
the imperfections you obsess over
in the mirror.

Who cares if you lose
the ones you thought would
stay in your life forever?
Better ones await you.

Anxiety will kick your ass;
just kick it right back.

Be grateful;
the world is all yours.

Be a little selfish;
there are only so many
pieces of yourself to give away
before there's nothing left of your soul.

Stop being so hard on yourself;
you will get there—
baby steps.

You are beautiful.
You are brave.
You are loved.

Clear Vision

When shades of black and white dye the sky above, and
Angel kisses illuminate the clouds that groan to the pulse of the
    breeze;
When the air drips with unspoken insincerity, and
The world's cruelty becomes too deafening—
Your mind salvages my detaching euphoria, and
Your heart opens my eyes to an infatuation I always craved.

Rising from the Ashes

You kindled the embers that set fire to my tears.

You lit the flame, purifying my soul.

You salvaged me from my own ruins, restoring the blaze that
will once again burn through my heart.

I will rise.

I will rise with you.

I Pray to You

I look up to the sky,

And pray to you.

Because I am not certain there is a God,

But I am certain there is you.

You will always be listening—

My beautiful angel.

Just One Last Embrace

In my dreams,

I dance with your ghost.

It is the only time

I can still feel your embrace.

When my eyes rest,

I fool myself into believing that heaven did not take you away.

My dreams are the only time when the whispering ache of
   losing you dims.

So I will continue dancing with your ghost for as long as I can.

All You Need Is You

Self-doubt should motivate you,
To prove yourself wrong.

You Kept Me Afloat

I was drowning from solitude for so long,

Until you came and drained the hollowness suffocating my lungs.

You held my head afloat amid the vicious waves,

Until I could catch my breath again.

And then you taught me how to swim.

Rejoice

Autumn,

When the sky drips with new beginnings

Leaves shed their sun-kissed skin,

And summer's carcass is laid to rest for another year.

Moving On, Moving Away

Skeletal remains of the city scatter on the ground below her,
A wreckage so stripped and raw that it leaves her saliva tasting
    like rust-filled faucets
dripping with remorse—taunting her to join the disarray of
    bodies that lay bare.
But turmoil is no longer stitched
    within her brain.
She no longer belongs to this city.
She exists only for herself now.

Taken for Granted

Dear moon and stars:
We blame you
For blackened nights,
For the men that form into wolves,
For the tears that paint our skin.

We blame you
For our deepest fears,
For sleepless nights,
For past mistakes.

But we should be thanking you
For displaying our demons,
For waking up our inner strength,
For shining a light
In our darkest times.

Teach Me Through the Wind

In the death of our loved ones,
We see what we try to run away from.

You look nothing like your mother;
You look just like your mother.
Beauty;
Misery.

Mother dearest,
Teach me how to walk away.
Show me how to make him beg.

Mother dearest,
Teach me how to be a woman.

I pray to you so much,
My tears taste just like you.

After the death of a loved one,
We are forced to stand still,
Even when the world is in chaos.

Worthy of the World

Why do you fear love and believe yourself unworthy?

Darling,
The moon and sun dance in your honour;
Women kneel at your feet, praying to be the one with the
    golden heart, while the golden heart belongs to you.

Hold yourself high for all to see that you are worthy of it all.

She Only Needs Herself

She will grow
with or without you.

You Are Greater Than Them

Baby girl,

Stop apologizing for the actions of others.

Here, Always

When sorrow is the only thing
Consuming your lungs,
Your flame has burnt out,
And your eyes scream exhaustion,
Let me be the shadow in your room;
Because sometimes light is not
The only thing we need.
Sometimes we need to know
That someone else is there.

You Lost a Masterpiece

I am a gallery of art,
But you decided to close your eyes
While walking my halls.

Too Good for This Earth

Her skin was sculpted from caramel,

Lips dripped of nectar,

Eyes glazed with freckles of the sky.

Dancing in the tall grass that tickled her sun-kissed fingertips,

She was everything you could imagine an angel was etched from,

And she chose you.

Concrete Love

Ribbons dance around his veins.

Raw skin peels away at his fingertips, where he bites at his uneasiness.

Sea waves envy his saliva as it pours down his throat.

Ashes tremble from his tongue.

Whenever his lips form your name, his voice sends goosebumps across your heart.

He is embroidered within your quilted skin, as long as he doesn't stop whispering your name.

Renewal

I tried to stay stagnant in the depths of familiarity.

I kept the butterflies confined within my mouth.

As their wings scraped against my tongue,

I hoped their beauty would dissolve into the lining of my skin.

Instead the butterflies grew.

As their tattered wings choked down my windpipe,

I could not contain the delicacy that began to form deep within.

I could not stay unchanging anymore,

So I allowed myself to transform.

Ten Stories Too High

Too much...
Grief in the marrow of these walls,
Tears causing structural damage,
Mold sprouted in the crevices of her heart.

Ten stories high,
And she could hear the cement singing her name.
The melody dripped down her spinal cord,
As the taste of the end seeped into her tongue.

She was mesmerized by the cracks that danced across the
    rigid cement—
The gray canvas lures her vision.

But she noticed a small flower blooming from the eroding
    cavities.
She chose to silence the screaming of her mind, because there
    was growth in decay, and hope for her.
She chose not to jump, but to heal instead.

You Are Yet to Blossom

Sometimes growth is not all in your roots,
But in the petals that have not yet bloomed.

This World Needs You

When you feel you're giving up,
Remember there are oceans singing your name,
Clouds breathing in your scent,
And flowers are not quite ready to sprout.

When you feel you're giving up,
Remember I need you,
This world needs you,
You need you.

With Love

The sky reminds me of you,
Awakening life into the skeleton of summer.
You've kissed the sunset, allowing pastels to merge amongst
    one another.

The sky reminds me of you
    in all its bliss.
You are the sky, which I envy because I am not there.

More Than Ordinary

A little broken,

glass shards of my heart

reflect sunbeams into the eyes of the ones who betrayed me.

What is broken

can be beautiful if you

salvage the remains to form something extraordinary.

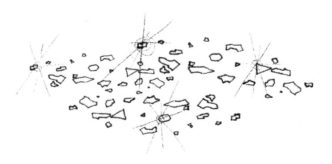

The City of Sheep

The sun kisses my cheek each morning, with gratitude and
   prosperity.

The pale sky greets me with fresh air and clear ambitions.

This world is not like the city I grew up in—
The city that tried to sculpt me into another dull body floating to
   the rhythm of its death wish.

Never-ending

If this pain and these memories are the only things I have left of
    you,
I will hold onto them so tightly my hands will grow scars.
And those scars will forever remind me of my unconditional love
    for you.

Here Is a Toast to You

As the leaves fall

Like nature's confetti,

And glasses rise to a new season,

Let the wind be your guide—

Free,

Loud,

Allowing autumn to carry you onwards.

This Is Your Future, Take Control

Darling,
stop letting your past
be the cement anchor
that sinks you
and drowns you
before your future
sees you fly.

Good Things Take Time

We think growth happens overnight.
We will wake up one morning, and the sun will beam
    contentment,
Lifting us above the soil, as our soul is no longer buried alive.

But actually, we begin to grow in fragments,
Until our growth consumes our remains,
And our healing overpowers the melancholy that was once
    forged into our minds.

We do not rush flowers to bloom,
So why do we rush ourselves?
To do so would be cruel,
Crushing tender sprouts
Amidst unrealistic expectations.

You Are Worth All the Skies' Lullabies

Your mind plays tricks on you:
Whispering through your skin,
Heavily resting on your shoulders,
Stitching scenarios into your brain,
Engraving the bone fragments of your skull with a lingering
promise of pain yet to be felt.

Your mind attacks you:
Not allowing the air to form inside your lungs,
Beating your heart against your ribcage so vigorously the bones
may snap.

Your mind harasses you:
Making you believe you are less than,
When truly you are the whole galaxy and more.

You are the stars that dance amongst the blackness,
The clouds that breathe lullabies into the sky.

Always with You

As three a.m. looms
And the stars lose their tender grip from the comfort of the
night,
Descending from the quilted sky,
And you feel unseen
From the eyes of those you adore,
Lost from your own soul,
I will be here.
I will always be here.

Breaking Free From Your Grip

To him,

I am just a broken heart with cracks patched by tenuous
glue;

One more break wouldn't hurt me, right?

To him,

I am a withering flower that he never had time to water.

To him,

I am never worthy of displaying;

Ignoring me was easier than dealing with the baggage of my
mind.

But to me,

He was everything I thought I wanted;

I let him break me,

Again and again,

Until I realized it was the unrealistic scenarios I made up in
my head

That made me believe he was the one.

To me,

I could then finally allow myself to be free.

Survivor

She wore sadness like a second layer of skin—
Each of her struggles removing another fragile layer,
Until only bones remain hollowed out.

She knew in order to survive,
She must regrow—
So she did.

Flowers sprouted from the depths of her lungs,
Moss cultivated,
Protecting her bones
Like a new skin.
Her sadness was replaced by gardens,
And she survived.

Fragile Soul of an Over-Thinker

Darling,

Do not let your stone mind shatter that glass soul of yours.

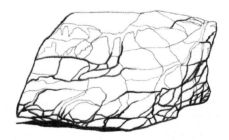

Clean Air

One day I will let you go.
No longer desiring to write about you,
My lungs will finally fill with air,
My drowning head will become afloat,
Temptations will disintegrate,
I will finally be able to breathe—
Breathe in clean air.

Minefield

Darling,

Is your pain severed into your skin?

Are you writing hatred against the flesh of your cheeks,

Fracturing the joints that hold your body together?

Your pain is more than skin-deep.

It has reached your glass heart,

Sending shards with each pump of blood crawling through your
body.

Darling,

Your pain will begin to damage every fragment of your being,

Unless you get a hold of the broken remains and begin securing
them back together.

You are your own savior;

Now Darling,

It is time to save yourself.

Evolving Happiness

Your smile is no longer made of glass,

Fragile and unstable,

But rather powerfully feeds on the carcass of your misery.

Your skeleton now nurtures growing buds of strength,

    blossoming rejoice.

Your smile, no longer temporary,

Lays indelibly along your face.

No Longer Mourning Over You

I vow to stop allowing you to stain my soul.
You are not my homeland anymore.

I vow to stop defending you,
As my tongue no longer has the space.

You do not bring me pain anymore.
My feelings for you are indifferent.

I am at peace with letting you go,
As I pursue a new homeland now.

Ignorance

I won't explain my heart,
Delicately articulating words to match the imprint of my soul,
To someone who chooses to ignore my voice.

She Is Everything And More

She is skin and bones
with so much soul to give.

Sketch Me into the Sky

You paint the sky
when you whisper my name.

Thank You

My friends hold my head afloat when I forget how to swim.

My friends plant seeds within my brain, nurturing me until I
blossom.

My friends know my thoughts are rotting, and gently remove the
decaying debris.

My friends are my life preservers.

He Deserves More
than the World

My father gave his two children all of his heart, all of his soul, all
    that we needed to grow.

He was our father, our mother, and the one who stitched us
    back together.

When he lost his wife, his soulmate, he did not let his heart
    disintegrate;
He was strong enough to put us first, even while drowning.

He is everything and more to me.

Dedicated to You

My wounds are the reason I started writing poetry.
I never wanted others to feel the pain I felt.

But I have come to realize I carried false hope.
The inevitable has happened,
And many endure wounds greater than mine.

So I write poetry for you now, darling,
So my words can begin to heal your mind, your heart, your
   traumas.

Uprooting

My bones chill,

As mother nature breathes in my ear to let go.

Your face blurs into the morning breeze.

Your voice no longer shivers through my stomach like withered
flowers.

I don't think I would recognize your voice,

Even if it screamed my name.

My skin has let your memory go.

I have let your memory go.

Rise to the Sky

Keep your head up;
The ground will not teach you to fly.

Manifest Your Success

I will be more than my past,

More than my mind has made me believe I am.

I will succeed,

Not to prove anyone wrong

Except for myself.

Seeing Clearly

When you remove the tainted
lens that blinds you of the truth,
You will begin to see
All the beauty you deserve.

Keep Believing in Myself

Lately my pen and I have been fighting about how to fill these
empty pages.
Is the battle eroding my brain worth the scars that line this
book?

It has to be,
As it is the only thing saving me from my inner misery.

Success Will Suffocate
the Envious

Stay away from the people who make you feel unworthy—
Unworthy of friendship, of love, of yourself.
Let them choke on your success.

The Strong Wouldn't Dare
to Leave You, Darling

You may be wondering why
They put their entire heart into the person they begin seeing
   after you,
While you still grasp the tiny part they left inside of you.
Why didn't they mourn over the loss of you?
Instead they found someone new.

Just know that they broke you,
But the broken always rises higher than the weak.

Words Are Her Savior

Poetry is engraved under her tongue—
Dripping off her lips,
Engulfing her mind.
It is the way she escapes
When she feels cemented to a dull life.
Poetry has become her;
She has become poetry.

Pain Sprouted Rejoice

When you left me,
I thought I would never breathe again,
Thought my tears would never stop running.

I wanted so badly to believe you would return to me,
Mend the aches that bound my body to my bed.

But time sang a differently lullaby,
And you never came back.

I could inhale the air that is no longer tainted in sorrow;
You sprouted a flower in me that outgrew you,
And for that I am thankful.

Beacon

You are my lighthouse,
When I am drowning in darkness.
You guide me to my shore.

You No Longer Thread
My Heart Together

I have removed your grasp around my throat.

You can no longer suffocate me,

As you have no more power over me.

I Am Proud of You

If you have survived your rock bottom,

I am proud of you,

Because no one will really know the darkness you felt.

No one will know the anchor attached to your soul was sinking
   you to the depths of the sea.

No one will know how your lungs are filled with hopelessness.

But you made it,

And I can see your light.

Your head is now afloat.

You can breathe;

You are a survivor.

Always Love Harder

I have found myself apologizing for the way I loved others—
  how I gave everyone all of me.
I was apologizing to men who got scared, because they had
  never received love so intensely.
I sensed their weakness as soon as their lips poured my name.
Their eyes glazed with insecurity, because they knew damn well
  they could never hold the amount of love I have in a single
  cell in their entire being.
I no longer apologize for the depth of my love,
And neither should you.

A Meadow of Flowers Now
Grow Under My Name

I spent years hating my name,

Wishing I could change it to something different—

Until you came along.

Then my name made droplets against your lips,

Like dew on a flower petal in mid-May—

Your voice sang my name like you needed it to survive.

I spent years wanting to change my name,

Until you came along

And sang it a different way.

You Radiate Eminence

You put your own pieces back together,
And that in itself is truly powerful.
You picked yourself up from the ground
More times than I can count.
You fed yourself love and illuminated your soul.

Darling,
You have done that,
All alone.
You are paramount.

Green Is Green No Matter the Shade

I like to people watch,

Take in their aura,

Imagine their grass is greener than mine,

That they live in a beautiful, white, picket-fenced house,

With a dog and three kids,

A loving partner,

And happiness that escapes their skin.

But I water my own grass;

It's a shade of green.

So who's to say they don't look at me,

And imagine my grass is as lovely as theirs?

I Have Risen from My Grave

My bones are the remnants of a graveyard
Where I once laid buried in soil.
The girl I once knew
No longer exists within the dirt,
But rises amongst the sky.

I Hope My Words
Sprout Prosperity

The purpose of my poetry
is to turn tears
into words—
mine and yours.

Paint the World with Your Grace

The sunset could not paint
The sky that glistens above,
If it were not for the beauty of your soul.

You Are Stronger than Yourself

Darling,
Your mind is wrong.

You belong in this beautiful world.

Your drizzle of self-destruction
Makes you capable of conquering the bruised beast
That tries to dominate your soul.

When Helping You,
I Help Myself

I write to you
The words that I wish I whispered
To myself—
When I grieved the loss of the happiness that once existed
  within my soul.

Breaking My Heart Free

One day, you will realize

I sacrificed my entire heart for you.

You will realize

How much happiness I brought you.

But I will be free,

And you will be left in misery.

How to Survive a Heartbreak

1. Cry, cry until there is no water draining from your eyes.
2. Rest, let your mind and soul drip into any amount of sleep it can.
3. Delete their pictures, erase their contacts. They are not reaching out. Why should you?
4. Miss them, bathe in the pain and hurt, and allow yourself to break down.
5. Cry again. It is okay to be broken.
6. Buy that one thing you have always wanted but didn't think you deserved. You deserve it, darling.
7. Go outside; bask in the sunlight as it replenishes your skin.
8. Breathe, let your lungs fill up with clean air.
9. Get rid of their shit. Burn it, return it.
10. The hardest one of all: love yourself. When they made you feel unlovable, it shows more about their character than yours. Love your tears and your golden heart. Love your pain and embrace your bruised soul. This won't last forever, but it may last for a while, so why not learn to love your own company? Give yourself the love you gave others, and watch yourself transform.

Rest in Forgiveness

My mind shutters away the peace,
Forcing me to remember pain,
Locking me in my own chains, shackled to misery.

Mourning the structural damage of my brain,
My memory dissipates each day.

This disease is eroding my soul,
But to heal I must forgive myself:
Forgive the darkness that envelopes my heart,
Forgive myself for isolating my bones against the world.

I must rest
In my own forgiveness.

You Are Strength

You will not chase;
You will be chased.
You will not fight;
You will be fought for.
You are worthy;
Stop choosing them
Before you choose yourself.

Let Me Drown Your Depression

Your vision is distorted by this fantasy
That this disease will not haunt your shadows.
Your lungs drown in envy,
As I watch the thistles grow your soul heavy.
Darling, there is so much more to this world than darkness—
So much grace for you to encounter—
But your brain whispers to me that you are homesick.
And the transparent river drowning all hope screams out your
     name.
You are a puppet to your own mind,
While it wraps its slender fingers around your heart strings
And begs for you to dive in,
Only to watch you sink deeper into its misery.
I can hear you.
I know there is so much more of you to be told.
Darling, let me grab hold of your drenched pain
Allow me to prove your worth.
It is not how long you can hold your breath under water,
But how you resurface from the agony.

I Will Not Kiss Your Feet Like the Others

He was spoiled,

In the eyes of his family he was a saint.

His empty words dripped from his tongue like honey—

So easily,

Smoothly.

But I do not taste honey;

I taste poison.

I see a young boy insecure in his own skin,

Hurting others to hide his own pain,

And I can no longer be his safeguard.

I will let go,

Because not all wounds can be fixed, especially those he
   repeatedly chooses to re-open.

She Is Someone to
Be Remembered

Her soul is why
hurricanes are named after people.

Darling,

If you are reading this, I know you have felt pain.

You have felt the world collapse on your brain,

And your heart has crumbled under too much weight.

From the bottom of my heart,

I am sorry.

I am sorry that depression is wired within your veins,

And that you walk past mirrors without being able to stomach
the reflection.

I am sorry someone with half your heart made you feel less
worthy,

Although I can see your worth.

Darling,

You are the stars that dance across this galaxy.

You are worthy of love as deep as the sea.

I hope when you have read this book,

You realize you are not alone.

I am here for you through pages,

With love and a gentle pen.

Allow me to steal some of that pain away.

Printed in Great Britain
by Amazon

20171511R00127